A Spelling Dictionary for Beginning Writers

Book 1

A Resource for Independent Writing

by Gregory Hurray

EDUCATORS PUBLISHING SERVICE

Cambridge and Toronto

Printed in the U.S.A.
ISBN 0-8388-2056-5

03 04 05 06 07 CUR 08 07 06 05 04

A Message to Teachers

This book is predicated on a very simple idea: children should be given access to the correct spellings of words they need in their writing. In the early grades, kindergarten through grade two, this turns out to be a fairly small number of words. According to studies by researchers such as E. Horn, Dewey, Fries, Rinsland, Fitzgerald, and others, a list of approximately 1,000 words accounts for nearly 90% of the words children in grades one and two commonly use in their stories, letters, and compositions. Unfortunately, many of the words used most frequently by young writers have irregular spellings: *does, was, said, pretty, one, once, many, been, there, are, put, they, would, what, friend,* and a host of other words used by children the first day they pick up a pencil or dictate a story to an adult. Words like these with unpredictable ("unencodable") spellings cannot be sounded out; they must be recalled from memory, retrieved from a book or chart, or written down by a teacher.

While academicians argue about the correct time to wean kids away from invented spellings, most educators agree that this should happen sometime in the first year of school. It is the experience of the author that most young writers not only want to spell words correctly, but willingly take on the responsibility for looking up the correct spellings of words when they are given the opportunity to do so, and when this endeavor is regarded as valuable and worthy by the adults around them.

Therefore, this book can be viewed as a tool to serve a dual purpose: (1) to give children a means to spell words correctly (and verify the accuracy of their very often ingenious guesses) and (2) to relieve the teacher of the burden of writing down, for each of twenty or twenty-five students, the correct spelling of every unfamiliar word the child asks to have spelled.

Unlike most beginning dictionaries, which often contain more than 10,000 entries and run to 500 or more pages, this volume is designed for maximum efficiency and use by the six- or seven-year-old student. It contains approximately 1,400 of the words most frequently used by children in kindergarten through second grade*, including a number of inflected forms placed next to their respective root words (*come/coming, swim/swimming,* for example) for the purpose of promoting in the student an awareness of suffix transformations. The Word Bank, found in the back of the book, includes a mini-thesaurus containing synonyms and replacements for words like *then, big, small, good/nice/great, went/ran,* and *said,* as well as handy reference lists of words grouped around specific themes such as numbers; colors; days, months, and seasons; sports and games; food; clothing; school; home; and family. Not all the words in the Word Bank are listed alphabetically. Some appear in order of frequency of use, making them more readily accessible to students.

Throughout, the intent has been to give students an opportunity to take responsibility for their own learning, to give them a chance to test out their emerging knowledge of English orthography, to encourage the development of good spelling habits from the very first day of composition work, and to make the classroom teacher's job as a promoter of good writing practices an easier one. To the extent that we succeed in each of these endeavors, our time will be well spent.

---

*Word choices for the Spelling Dictionary were based on published research as well as the author's research and experience in the public schools.

How to Use This Book

Explain to students that this is a list of words that children their age use over and over when writing—words like *the, said, because, beautiful, brought, always*. Tell them that because it contains only those words which they are most likely to use, it is shorter and easier to use than a regular dictionary. Encourage them to keep this book on their desks when they write, and to look up the spellings of all words they're not sure of.

Tell students that this dictionary is theirs to keep, and that it is okay to write in it. Point out that space has been provided at the bottom of each page for them to add words of their own. Discuss how they can also practice alphabetizing skills as they add words by inserting them in the space available between those already listed.

Show students the Word Bank in the back of the book, including the mini-thesaurus containing synonyms for *then, big, small,* and other words which tend to be overused. Explain that other words are grouped around a common theme (colors, numbers, the family, etc.) and that most are alphabetized. Ask students how they might use this section. (To find the spellings of less common words like *visor* or *gymnastics;* to find the spellings of months, holidays, and numbers; and to spark ideas for using specific words like *beige* and *magenta*.)

Encourage students to develop a strategy for finding the correct spellings of unfamiliar words, a strategy that includes the following steps:

1. Try to sound out the word.

2. Look for it in this dictionary.

3. If it is here, mark it as a word that you've needed and have looked up.

4. If it is not here, ask your teacher for the first few letters. Then look it up in a regular dictionary and write it in this book for future reference.

You may wish to have students practice using this book by looking up a few sample words such as *because, school, tree, shopping* (listed with its root form, *shop*), and *hear* and *here* (point out that meaning clues are given for homonyms). Have students circle each word they look up to make it easier to find a second time.

Dear Student,

This book contains a list of words that beginning writers use over and over in their writing.

It is shorter and easier to use than a regular dictionary. Use it whenever you need to check the spelling of a word you're not sure of. As you will discover, there is room on each page to add your own words.

Also, the back of the book contains a Word Bank, which your teacher will explain to you.

Write well and write often!

Best wishes,

A. A. Hurray

Gregory Hurray

P.S. Please feel free to suggest any words you think should be in this book. You can write to me in care of Educators Publishing Service, P.O. Box 9031, Cambridge, MA 02138-1089.

Contents

Dictionary

A

able

about

above

accident

across

act

add

addition

address

adventure

afraid

after

afternoon

afterward

again

against

age

ago

ahead

air

airplane

airport

alike

alive

all

allow, allowed

all right

almost

alone

along

a lot

already

_____

_____

_____

_____

_____

_____

_____

_____

_____

also

although

always

am

America, American

among

and

angry

animal

another

answer, answered

any

anybody

anyone

anything

anyway

apple

April

are [You are reading now.]

aren't

argue, argument

arithmetic

arm

around

art

as

ask, asked

asleep

astronaut

at

ate [I ate lunch.]

August

aunt

automatic

autumn

awake

away

awful

awhile

B

baby

back

bad

bag

_____

_____

_____

bake

ball

balloon

bank

barn

baseball

basement

basket

basketball

bath

battle

be

beach

bear [Don't feed the bear.]

beast

beat

beautiful

became

because

become

bed

bedroom

been [Where have you been?]

before

began

begin, beginning

behind

believe

bell

belong

below

beside

best

bet

better

between

beyond

bicycle

big, biggest

bike

bird

birthday

bit

bite

black

_____

_____

_____

_____

blanket	born	breakfast
bleed	borrow	breath
blew [The wind blew.]	boss	breathe
blocks	both	breeze
blood	bottle	bridge
blow	bottom	bright
blue [blue sky]	bought	bring
board [wooden board]	bow	broke, broken
boat	bowl	brother
body	box	brought
boil	boy	brown
bomb	branch	build, building
bones	brave	built
book	bread	burn
bored, boring	break [to break something]	bury
_____	_____	_____
_____	_____	_____
_____	_____	_____

bus

bush

business

busy

but

butter

buy [to buy food]

by [made by Joan]

bye [good-bye]

C

cage

cake

call, called

calm

came

camera

camp

can

candy

cannot

can't

cap

captain

car

card

care, careful

carry, carried

cassette

castle

cat

catch

caught

cave

ceiling

celebrate

center

cents [5 cents]

cereal

chain

chair

chance

change

charge

_____

_____

_____

_____

_____

_____

_____

_____

_____

chase	circle	coat
cheap	circus	coffee
check	city	cold
cheek	class	collect, collection
cheer	clay	color, colorful
cheese	clean	comb [to comb your hair]
chew	clear	come, coming
chicken	climb, climbed	comfortable
chief	clock	company
child	close, closing	complete
children	closet	computer
chocolate	clothes	contest
choose [to choose a gift]	cloud	cook
chose [We chose sides.]	clown	cookies
church	coach	cool
Christmas		

copy, copied

corn

corner

cost

costume

cotton

cough

could

couldn't

count

country, countries

couple [a couple of . . .]

course [of course]

cousin

cover

_____

_____

_____

_____

cow

cowboy

crayon

crazy

cream

cried

crooked

cross

crowd, crowded

crown

cruel

cry, crying

cup

cut

cute

cuddley

_____

_____

_____

D

dad, daddy

dance

danger

dangerous

dare

dark

date

daughter

day

dead

dear [Dear John,]

death

December

decide

_____

_____

_____

_____

deep

deer [the animal]

delicious

dentist

desk

dessert [What's for <u>dessert</u>?]

destroy, destroyed

did

didn't

die, died

different

difficult

dinner

dinosaur

dirt, dirty

disappear

dish, dishes

disk (or disc)

do, doing

doctor

does

doesn't

dog

doll

dollar

done

don't

door

double

down

downstairs

dozen

dragon

draw, drawing

dream

dress, dressed

drink

drive

drop, dropped

drum

dry, dried

drying

duck

dumb

during

_____

_____

_____

_____

_____

_____

_____

_____

_____

_____

_____

_____

E

each

ear

early

earth

east

easy, easily

eat, eating

edge

egg

eight [8]

either

electric

electricity

elephant

Easter

eleven

else

empty

end

engine

enjoy, enjoyed

enormous

enough

enter

environment

escape

especially

even

evening

even though

ever

every

everybody

everyone

everything

everywhere

exactly

excellent

except

excited

exercise

experience

explain

explore

eye [Blink your right eye.]

F

fabulous

face

fair

fairy

fall

false

family

famous

fantastic

far

farm, farmer

farther

fast

fat

father

fault

favorite

feed

feel, feeling

feet

fell

felt

fence

few

field

fifth

fight

figure

fill

finally

find

fine

finger

finish, finished

fire

first

fish, fishing

five

fix, fixed

flag

flavor

flew

float

floor

_____

_____

_____

_____

_____

_____

_____

_____

_____

_____

_____

_____

flour [bake with flour]

flower [flower in a garden]

fly, flying

fold

folks

follow, followed

food

fool

foot

football

for [a gift for you]

forest

forget

forgot

fought

found

four [4]

fourth [fourth grade]

fox

free

freeze

fresh

Friday

friend, friendly

frighten, frightened

frog

from

front

frozen

fruit

full

fun

funny

fur [an animal's fur]

furniture

future

G

game

garden

gas

gate

gave

gentle

get, getting

_____

_____

_____

_____

ghost

giant

gift

gigantic

girl

give, giving

glad

glass

glove

go, going

goal

goalie

goes

gold

gone

good

good-bye

got

grade

grandfather

grandma

grandmother

grandpa

grass

gray

great

green

grew

ground

group

grow

guard

guess, guessed

guest [a guest for dinner]

gum

guy

gym

H

had

hair

half

hall

Halloween

hand

_____

_____

_____

_____

_____

_____

_____

_____

_____

_____

_____

_____

handle

happen, happened

happily

happy, happiest

hard

hardly

has

hat

hate

haunted

have, having

haven't

hay [Horses eat hay.]

he

head

healthy

hear [I hear the bell now.]

heard [I heard you.]

heart

heat

heaven

heavy

hello

help, helped

her

here [Here it is!]

herself

hey [Hey, you!]

hi [Hi. How are you?]

hide

high [high and low]

hike

hill

him

himself

his

hit

hockey

hold

hole [a hole in the ground]

holiday

home

homework

hop, hopped

hope, hoping

_____

_____

_____

horn

horrible

horse

hospital

hot

hotel

hour [an hour from now]

house

how

however

huge

human

hundred

hungry

hunt

hurry, hurried

hurt

husband

I

I

ice

ice cream

idea

I'll

I'm

imagine

immediately

important

impossible

in

inch, inches

ink

insect

inside

instead

interesting

into

invite, invited

is

island

isn't

it

it's [it is]

_____

_____

_____

_____

its [The dog bit its tail.]

I've

J

jar

juice, juicy

jump, jumped

June

just

K

keep

kept

kick, kicked

kids

kill, killed

kind, kindness

king

kiss, kissed

kitchen

kite

kitten

kitty

knee

knew [I thought I knew how.]

knife

knock, knocked

knot [to tie a knot!]

know [I know the answer.]

L

ladder

lady, ladies

lake

lamb

lamp

land, landed

large, largest

laser

last

late

later

laugh, laughed

lawn

lay, laid

_____

_____

_____

_____

_____

_____

_____

_____

_____

lazy

lead

league

leak

learn

least [at least]

leave, leaving

left

leg

less

lesson

let

let's [Let's go!]

letter

library

lie, lying

life

lift

light

like

line

lion

listen

little

live, living, lived

load

loan

lock

lonely

lonesome

long

look, looked

loose [The dog is loose.]

lose [to lose your money]

lost

lots [We had lots of fun.]

loud

love, lovely

low

lucky, luckily

lunch

M

machine

mad [I'm mad at you!]

_____

_____

_____

_____

made [I made it myself.]

magic

mail

mailman

main [the main idea]

make, making

mall [shopping mall]

man

many

mark

marry, married

math

matter

may

maybe

me

mean

meanwhile

meat [to eat meat]

medicine

meet [to meet your friends]

men

met

middle

might

mile

milk

million

mind [Do you mind?]

mine [Is it yours or mine?]

minute

miss, missed

mistake

mix, mixed

mom, mommy

moment

Monday

money

monkey

monster, monstrous

month

moon

more

morning

most

_____

_____

_____

_____

_____

_____

_____

_____

_____

mother

motor

mountain

mouse

mouth

move, moving

movie, movies

Mr.

Mrs.

Ms.

much

mud

music

must

my

myself

mystery, mysterious

N

name, named

Native American

nature, natural

near, nearly

neat [It's so neat!]

necessary

neck

need

neighbor, neighborhood

nest

never

new [a new toy]

newspaper

next

nice, nicest

nickel

night [day and night]

nine

ninth

no [yes or no]

nobody

noise

noon

no one

north

_____

_____

_____

_____

nose

not

nothing

notice

now

number

nurse

nuts

O

ocean

o'clock

of

off

office

often

oh

oil

okay

old

on

oncc

one [1]

only

open, opened

or

orange

order

ordinary

other

ought

our [our house]

ourselves

out

outside

oven

over

own

P

package

page

pail [a pail of water]

pain [pain in the neck]

paint

_____

_____

_____

_____

_____

_____

_____

_____

_____

pair [a pair of pants]

pants

paper

parade

parents

park

part

party

pass

passed [I passed the test.]

past [It's past your bedtime.]

pay, paid

peace, peaceful

pear [Eat a pear.]

pen

pencil

penny, pennies

people

perfect

period

person

pet

phone

piano

pick, picked

picnic

picture

pie

piece [a piece of pie]

pig

pile

pink

place

plain [not fancy]

plan, planned

plane [airplane]

plant

plastic

play, played, playing

pleasant

please

pleasure

plenty

plus

pocket

_____

_____

_____

_____

_____

_____

_____

_____

_____

point

poison

police

pollution

pond

pony, ponies

poor [having no money]

pop

porch

possible

potato, potatoes

pound

pour [to pour a drink]

practically

practice, practicing

pray

present

pretty, prettiest

price

prince

princess

principal [school principal]

principle

private

prize

probably

problem

program

promise

proud

prove

pudding [chocolate pudding]

pull, pulled

pumpkin

puppy, puppies

purple

push, pushed

put, putting

Q

quart

quarter

queen

question

_____

_____

_____

_____

_____

_____

_____

_____

_____

_____

_____

_____

quick, quickly

quiet, quietly

quit [We quit the game.]

quite [I ate quite a lot.]

R

rabbit

race

radio

rain

rainbow

ran

rang

rather

reach

read, reading

ready

real

realized

really

reason

receive

record

red

regular

remain

remember

replied

report

rest

restaurant

return, returned

ribbon

rice

rich

ride, riding

right [right/left; right/wrong]

ring

ripe

rise

river

road [a street]

robot

rock

_____

_____

_____

_____

rocket

rode [I rode my bike.]

roll, rolled

roof

room

root [tree root]

rope

rose [pink rose]

rough

round

row

rubber

rule

run, running

rush

_____

_____

_____

_____

S

sad

safe, safely

said

sail [sail a boat]

sale [It's on sale!]

salt

same

sand

sandwich

sang

sat

save

saw

say, saying

_____

_____

_____

_____

says

scare, scared

scary, scariest

school

science

scientist

scissors

score

scream

sea [seashore]

search

season

seat

second

secret

scorpions

_____

_____

_____

see [I see you.]

seem, seemed

seen [Have you seen my cat?]

sell

send

sense [It makes no sense.]

sent [She sent me a letter.]

sentence

separate

serious

serve

set

settle

seven

several

shade

shadow

shake

shape

share

sharp

she

sheep

shell

shine, shining

ship

shirt

shoe, shoes

shoot

shop, shopping

shore [seashore]

short

should

shoulder

shouldn't

shout

shove

shovel

show, showed

shower

shy

sick

side

sidewalk

sight

_____

_____

_____

_____

_____

_____

_____

_____

_____

_____

_____

_____

sign

silly

simple

since

sincerely

sing, singing

sister

sit, sitting

six

size

skate, skating

skin

sky

sled, sledding

sleep, sleeping

slept

slide

slow, slowly

small, smallest

smart

smash, smashed

smell

smile

smoke

smooth

snack [to eat a snack]

snake [animal without legs]

sneak

sneakers

sneeze

snow, snowing

so [I ate so much!]

soap

soccer

soft, softly

sold

soldier

some

somebody

someone

something

sometimes

somewhere

son [son and daughter]

song

_____

_____

_____

_____

soon

sorry

sort of

sound

soup

sour

south

space

speak

special

spell, spelling

spend

spent

spider

spoil, spoiled

spoke

spooky

sport

spread

spring

square

squeak

squeeze

squirrel

stairs

stand

star

stare [to stare at someone]

start

state

station

stay, stayed

steal [to steal something]

step, stepped

stereo

stick

still

stomach

stone

stood

stop, stopped

store

storm

story, stories

stove

_____

_____

_____

_____

straight

strange

straw

stream

street

string

strong

stuck

study, studying

stuff

stupid

subject

such

sudden, suddenly

sugar

suggest

suit

summer

sun, sunny

Sunday

super

supper [What's for supper?]

suppose, supposed

sure

surprise, surprised

swallow, swallowed

sweater

sweet

swim, swimming

swing

sword

T

table

tag

tail [a cat's tail]

take, taking

tale [a fairy tale]

talk, talking

tall

taste

taught [She taught me a lesson.]

teach

teacher

team

_____

_____

_____

_____

_____

_____

_____

_____

_____

_____

_____

_____

tear [a teardrop; to tear paper]

teeth

telephone

television

tell

ten

terrible

test

than [I'm taller than you.]

thank

that

the

theater

their [their house]

them

themselves

then [. . . and then we left.]

there [Look over there!]

these

they

they're [they are]

thick

thief, thieves

thing

think, thinking

third

thirsty

this

those

though [Even though . . . .]

thought

thousand

three

threw [I threw the ball.]

throat

through [through the door]

throw [to throw a ball]

thrown [The ball was thrown.]

thumb

Thursday

ticket

tie, tied, tying

tiger

tight

till [Wait till tomorrow.]

_____

_____

_____

_____

_____

_____

_____

_____

_____

time

tiny, tiniest

tip

tired

tissue

to [I went to the store.]

toad

toast

today

toe [big toe]

together

told

tomorrow

tongue

tonight

too [I ate too much, too.]

took

tool

tooth

top

tore [I tore my coat.]

torn

total

touch

tough

tour [to go on a tour]

tow [to tow a car]

toward

town

toy

trade

train

travel

treasure

tree

trick, tricky

tried

trip, tripped

trouble

truck

true

trunk

truth

try, trying

Tuesday

_____

_____

_____

_____

_____

_____

_____

_____

_____

_____

_____

_____

turkey

turn, turned

turtle

TV

twelve

twenty

twice

two [2]

unless

until

unusual

up

upon [Once upon a time . . . .]

upstairs

us

use, used, using

used to

usually

valley

valuable

vegetable

very

view

village

visit

visitor

voice

U

ugly

uncle

under

understand

V

vacation

valentine

W

wagon

wait [Wait for me!]

wake

_____

_____

_____

_____

_____

_____

_____

_____

_____

_____

_____

_____

walk, walked

wall

want

war [to fight a war]

warm

warn

was

wash

wasn't

waste [Don't waste time!]

watch, watched

water

wave

way [Which way do we go?]

we

weak [not strong]

wealthy

wear [to wear a hat]

weather [sunny weather]

week [7 days in a week]

weekend

weight [How much did it weigh?]

weighed [It weighed a ton.]

weird

welcome

well

went

were [Where were you?]

we're [we are: We're happy.]

west

wet

what

whatever

wheel

when

whenever

where [Where do you live?]

whether [whether or not]

which [Which one is it?]

while

white

who

whole [the whole thing]

why

wide

_____   _____   _____

_____   _____   _____

_____   _____   _____

_____   _____   _____

wife

wild

will

win

wind

window

wing

winter

wise

wish, wished, wishes

witch [Halloween witch]

with

without

woke

wolf, wolves

woman [one woman]

women [two or more women]

won [We won the game.]

wonder, wondering

wonderful

won't

wood [to chop wood]

woods

wool

word

wore [She wore gloves.]

work

world

worm

worn

worried

worry

worse [worse than ever]

worst [the worst one]

worth

would [Would you like help?]

wouldn't

wrap [to wrap a gift]

wreck, wrecked

write, writing

written

wrong

wrote

_____

_____

_____

_____

_____

_____

_____

_____

_____

_____

_____

_____

X	yell	your [your own book]
Xerox	yellow	you're [you are]
	yes	Yours truly,
Y	yesterday	
yard	yet	Z
yawn	you	zoo
year	young	

---------------   ---------------   ---------------

---------------   ---------------   ---------------

---------------   ---------------   ---------------

---------------   ---------------   ---------------

Word Bank

Mini-Thesaurus

Words for *then*

next	a short time later	when that was done
after that	at that moment	shortly thereafter
later	afterward	now
a few minutes later	following that	finally
a moment later		

Words for *big*

large	immense	mighty
huge	tremendous	colossal
gigantic	humongous (slang)	bulky
giant-sized	monstrous	grand
great	massive	vast
enormous	mammoth	gargantuan

Words for *small* or *little*

tiny	minute	microscopic
teeny	mini-	undersized
teeny-weeny	wee	minuscule
itsy-bitsy	slight	diminutive
miniature	puny	

Words for *good*, *nice*, **or** *great*

fabulous	super	charming
fantastic	superb	exciting
wonderful	amazing	extraordinary
terrific	excellent	outstanding
remarkable	lovely	memorable
incredible	exceptional	perfect
marvelous	beautiful	stupendous
magnificent	fine	flawless
spectacular	splendid	breathtaking
awesome	delightful	

Words for *went* or *ran*

walked	trotted	sped
hurried	galloped	slid
rushed	stomped	limped
raced	scurried	glided
flew	bolted	moved
dashed	hustled	headed
sprinted	slithered	left
charged	skipped	departed
darted	fled	bounded
scampered		

Words for *asked*

begged	questioned
pleaded	requested
demanded	inquired

Words for *answered*

replied	shot back
responded	snapped back

Words for *said*

yelled	remarked	declared
screamed	screeched	boasted
shouted	shrieked	repeated
cried out	barked	squeaked
called out	snorted	snickered
moaned	snapped	stated
explained	squawked	begged
laughed	muttered	pleaded
chuckled	ordered	bellowed
mumbled	hissed	blurted out
sobbed	insisted	boasted
whispered	interrupted	commanded
whined	announced	asserted
exclaimed	commented	demanded
exploded	mentioned	murmured
roared	stated	stammered

Theme Words

The Calendar

Days of the Week	Months of the Year	Holidays
Monday	January	Labor Day
Tuesday	February	Halloween
Wednesday	March	Columbus Day
Thursday	April	Thanksgiving
Friday	May	Veterans Day
Saturday	June	Hanukkah (or Chanukah)
Sunday	July	Christmas
Seasons	August	New Year's Day
summer	September	Groundhog Day
fall (autumn)	October	Valentine's Day
winter	November	Martin Luther King, Jr.'s Birthday
spring	December	Presidents' Day
		Memorial Day
		Fourth of July (Independence Day)

Numbers

1	one	100	one hundred	
2	two	1,000	one thousand	
3	three	1,000,000	one million	
4	four	1st	first	
5	five	2nd	second	
6	six	3rd	third	
7	seven	4th	fourth	
8	eight	5th	fifth	
9	nine	6th	sixth	
10	ten	7th	seventh	
11	eleven	8th	eighth	
12	twelve	9th	ninth	
13	thirteen	10th	tenth	
14	fourteen	20th	twentieth	
15	fifteen	30th	thirtieth	
16	sixteen			
17	seventeen			
18	eighteen			
19	nineteen			
20	twenty			
30	thirty			
40	forty			
50	fifty			
60	sixty			
70	seventy			
80	eighty			
90	ninety			

Colors

aqua
beige
black
blue
brown
chartreuse
copper
gold
gray
green
lavender
magenta
maroon
orange
peach
pink
purple
red
rose
silver
tan
turquoise
violet
white
yellow

Clothes

backpack

bathing suit

bathrobe

belt

bikini

blouse

blue jeans

boots

button

cap

clogs

coat

collar

cotton

cuff

down

dress

earmuffs

flannel

fleece

glasses

gloves

hat

hood

jacket

jeans

jumper

jumpsuit

khakis

leotard

loafers

mittens

nightgown

nylon

overalls

pajamas

pants

parka

plaid

pocket

polyester

poncho

raincoat

robe

sandals

scarf

shirt

shoes

shorts

skirt

slacks

sleeve

slippers

snaps

sneakers

snowsuit

socks

stockings

suit

sunglasses

suspenders

sweater

sweatpants

sweatshirt

swimsuit

T-shirt

tie

tights

trousers

tuxedo

underwear

Velcro™

vest

visor

wool

zipper

School

abacus	chalk	eraser
absent	chalkboard	excuse
add	charts	exercise
addition	chorus	experiment
afternoon	circle	field trip
alphabet	class	filmstrip
animals	classroom	fingerpaint
answer	clay	fire drill
aquarium	closet	first grade
arithmetic	coloring	fish
art	computer	fish tank
assignment	crayons	flag
auditorium	cubby	floor
bathroom	Cuisenaire™ rods	folder
blocks	custodian	foot
board	desk	game
book	dice	geoboard
bottle	dictionary	gerbil
boxes	Dienes™ blocks	globe
brush	diorama	glue
bulletin board	disk (disc)	graph paper
bus	divide	guinea pig
cabinet	division	gym
cafeteria	dollhouse	hall
cage	draw	hallway
calculator	drinking fountain	hammer
cassette	early	hamster
centimeter	easel	holiday
chair	equipment	homeroom

School

homework	microscope	pledge [pledge of allegiance]
inch	monitor	poem
instrument	morning	poster
intercom	movie	poster paint
Internet	multiplication	principal
jungle gym	multiply	print
keyboard	music	problem
kindergarten	nails	program
language arts	name	project
late	needle	projector
learn	newspaper	puppets
Legos™	notebook	puzzle
letters	numbers	quiet
library	nurse	rabbit
lice	nursery school	read
lights	paint	reading
line	paintbrush	recess
locker	paper	record player
lunch	paper clip	report
lunchroom	papier-mâché	rubber band
magazine	paste	rug
magnet	pen	ruler
map	pencil	sandbox
marker	period	saw
materials	phonograph	schedule
math	pillow	science
medicine	play	scissors
meeting	Play-Doh®	screen
meter	playground	screwdriver

School

second grade	swing	
secretary	table	
sentence	tape	
shelf	tape recorder	
show and tell	teacher	
silent reading	terrarium	
sink	thread	
slide	thumbtack	
snack	tools	
soap	triangle	
social studies	TV	
software	typewriter	
spelling	vacation	
sports	video	
square	wall	
stage	water table	
stairs	Web site	
stapler	word	
story, stories	workbook	
student	workbench	
study	writing	
subject	yardstick	
subtract	yarn	
subtraction		

Family

aunt
babysitter
brother
child
children
cousin
dad, daddy
daughter
father
grandfather
grandma
grandmother
grandpa
guest
mom, mommy
mother
nanna
neighbor
nephew
niece
relatives
sister
son
stepbrother
stepfather
stepmother
stepsister
uncle

Home

address

air conditioner

apartment

appliances

attic

backyard

basement

bathroom

bathtub

bedroom

buffet

bureau

cabinets

ceiling

cellar

chair

closet

computer

condominium

couch

cushion

den

desk

dining room

dishwasher

door

doorbell

driveway

dryer

electrical outlet

elevator

fan

faucet

fireplace

floor

freezer

furniture

garage

garbage can

garbage disposal

garden

hallway

heater

house

kitchen

lamp

laser disc player

laundry room

light

living room

machines

microwave oven

mirror

oven

pantry

phone

piano

pillow

playroom

porch

radiator

radio

record player

refrigerator

roof

sewing machine

shower

sink

sofa

speakers

stairs

stereo

stove

study

switch

table

telephone

television, TV

toaster

toilet

trash

VCR

video cassette recorder

wall

washing machine

window

work room

yard

Word Bank

Sports and Games

archery	hide and seek	scavenger hunt
badminton	hiking	score
ball	hockey puck	scuba diving
baseball	hopscotch	skateboard
basketball	horseback riding	skates
bat	hunting	skating
bow and arrow	ice skating	ski, skis
bowling	in-line skating	skiing
boxing	jogging	sled, sledding
candlepins	judo	snorkel, snorkeling
canoe, canoeing	juggling	snowboard
cards	jump rope	soccer
checkers	karate	softball
chess	kickball	squash
chessboard	league	stickball
chess pieces	marathon	surfing
coach	mask	swimming
contest	mountain climbing	team
diving	Olympics	tennis
dominoes	paddle	tetherball
fencing	ping pong	toboggan
fishing	polo	track meet
flippers	practice	volleyball
football	racket	water skiing
game	racquetball	weight lifting
glove	rock climbing	wind surfing
goal	roller skating	wrestling
goalie	running	
gymnastics	sailing	

60

Weather

air
atmosphere
barometer
barometric pressure
blizzard
brisk
Celsius (C)
centigrade
chilly
climate
cloud
cold
cool
cyclone
degrees
dew
dew point
drizzle
fair
Fahrenheit (F)
flood
fog
forecast
freezing
frigid
frost
gust
hail
haze, hazy

hot
humid
humidity
hurricane
lightning
meteorologist
meteorology
mild
moisture
monsoon
muggy
precipitation
puddle
rain
sleet
smog
snow
storm
sunny
sweltering
temperature
thermometer
thunder
thunderstorm
tide
tornado
wave
weathervane
wind

Body Parts

abdomen
ankle
arm
belly
belly button
bone
calf
cheek
chest
chin
ear
elbow
eye
eyebrow
finger
fingernail
foot
forearm
forehead
hair
hand
head
heel
hip

Body Parts

joint

knee

knuckle

leg

limb

lip

moustache

mouth

muscle

navel

neck

nose

nostril

palm

shin

shoulder

skin

thigh

thumb

toe

tooth, teeth

torso

waist

wrist

Astronomy and Space

aeronautics

asteroid

astronaut

axis

black hole

capsule

cluster

comet

constellation

day

Earth

equinox

galaxy

gravity

jet plane

Jupiter

horizon

launch

magnetic field

Mars

Mercury

meteor

Milky Way

moon

nebula

Neptune

night

observatory

orbit

planet

Pluto

quasar

radio telescope

rocket, rocket science

rotate, rotation

satellite

Saturn

shuttle

solar system

solstice

spacecraft

space station

space suit

star

sun

supernova

telescope

universe

Uranus

Venus

Geography

Africa	field	province
Antarctica	forest	rain forest
Asia	glacier	reef
Australia	grassland	region
bay	gulf	reservoir
beach	gully	ridge
border	harbor	river
canal	iceberg	sea
canyon	island	shore
cape	jungle	south
cave	lagoon	South America
cavern	lake	spring
city	latitude	state
coast	lava flow	strait
continent	longitude	stream
continental shelf	mountain	swamp
country	north	terrain
county	North America	territory
cove	ocean	town
crater	park	tunnel
delta	pasture	valley
desert	peninsula	village
dune	plain	volcano
east	plateau	west
equator	pole	wetlands
erosion	pollution	woods
Europe	pond	
fault line	prairie	